A SOUVENIR GUIDE TO
ORKNEY

by
Charle˜

Third Edition

A Souvenir Guide to Orkney

Edition 3
Published by Charles Tait Photographic Ltd
Kelton, St Ola, Orkney KW15 1TR Tel 01856 873738 Fax 01856 875313
charles.tait@zetnet.co.uk   www.charles-tait.co.uk

This book is dedicated to my aunt, Margaret C Tait (1918-1999)

Text, design and layout © copyright Charles Tait Photographic Ltd
Photographs © copyright Charles Tait Photographic Ltd
Old Photographs from Charles Tait collection
Printing by Kine Italia, Italy
OS maps reproduced from Ordnance Survey mapping with permission of the
Controller of HMSO, © Crown Copyright Reserved 100035677

Front cover: Ring of Brodgar
ISBN 09517859 2 3

A SOUVENIR GUIDE to ORKNEY

COPYRIGHT © CHARLES TAIT 2007

CONTENTS

WELCOME TO ORKNEY

Aurora borealis from Wideford Hill

There is much to see and do in Orkney, and this guide is designed to help visitors find and appreciate the main sites of interest on the Mainland and other islands. The rich archaeological heritage of the islands is one of their prime attractions, but the soft green and fertile landscape, beautiful beaches, spectacular cliffs, abundant wildlife and above all friendly people are equally important in making up "Orkney".

Orkney lies just north of Mainland Scotland at around 59°N and comprises over 70 islands of which 17 or 18 are inhabited by about 21,000 people. The first written reference to the islands is by Pytheas the Greek in 325BC, but they have been inhabited for at least 6,000 years. The timeline from prehistory through historical times to the 21st century is continuous, making the division between past and present at times hard to discern.

Perhaps most famous for its exceptionally well-preserved Neolithic monuments, some of which now enjoy World Heritage status, Orkney has a wealth of other visitor attractions ranging from archaeological sites, local museums, the Highland Park Distillery and St Magnus Cathedral, to a diverse array of craft workshops and shops selling attractive local goods. Wildlife, especially birds, is another feature of Orkney not to be missed, whatever the season. This book aims to maximise the benefit of your visit, no matter how short.

The Old Red Sandstone rocks result in a combination of fertile agricultural land, most of which is used to raise Orkney's renowned grass-fed beef cattle, moorland and spectacular coastal fringes, making it a haven for many species of birds in every season, while in spring and Summer wild flowers are abundant.

The maritime climate combined with the relatively warm Atlantic Ocean, make the climate very equable, with snow and frost rare in winter. Equally, the temperature rarely exceeds 20 degrees in summer. Situated at the meeting point of the North Sea and Atlantic Ocean the islands are surrounded by waters abundant in fish and shellfish, adding to the wide variety of locally produced quality foods.

Whether the one arrives by air or sea at Kirkwall or by sea at Stromness, St Margaret's Hope or Burwick,

Orkney presents a strong contrast to the Highlands. Both towns are dominated by their winding main streets and harbours, while Kirkwall also has the imposing 12th century St Magnus Cathedral.

Both towns have excellent shops, hotels and eating places, as well as interesting museums and make goodbases from which to explore the rest of Orkney. Even on the shortest of visits there are several "must see" sites.

St Magnus Cathedral in Kirkwall dates from 1137

Good places to start are the Orkney Museum or the Highland Park Visitor Centre, with its excellent audiovisual, in Kirkwall, followed by a tour of the West Mainland taking in Maeshowe, the Ring of Brodgar and the Standing Stones and then Skara Brae. If time permits there are many more places which can be visited in a day.

On a longer visit it is strongly suggested that a visit should be made to at least one of the other inhabited islands, all of which are very accessible by ferry or aircraft. Each island has a character all of its own and all have interesting places to visit as well as accommodation and shops.

A good map is a great help in all such visits and the VisitOrkney produces a useful one which also includes Shetland. The Ordnance Survey 1:50,000 series covers Orkney in three sheets, and is recommended for all serious explorers. Most of the places mentioned in this book are signposted.

ORKNEY COUNTRYSIDE CODE

We are justly proud of our historic sites, wildlife and environment. Please help ensure that future visitors may enjoy them as much as you by observing these guidelines:

1. Always use stiles and gates and close gates after you.
2. Always ask permission before entering agricultural land.
3. Keep to paths and take care to avoid fields of grass and crops.
4. Do not disturb livestock.
5. Take your litter away with you and do not light fires.
6. Do not pollute water courses or supplies.
7. Never disturb nesting birds.
8. Do not pick wild flowers or dig up plants.
9. Drive and park with due care and attention - do not obstruct or endanger others.
10. Always take care near cliffs - particularly with children and pets.
11. Walkers should take adequate clothes, wear suitable footwear and tell someone of their plans.
12. Above all please respect the life of the countryside - leave only footprints, take only photographs and pleasant memories.

Notice: While most of the sites of interest are open to the public and have marked access, many are on private land. No right of access is implied in the description, and if in doubt it is always polite to ask. Also, while many roads and tracks are rights of way, not all are.

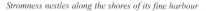
Stromness nestles along the shores of its fine harbour

A Tour of the Main Monuments

Orkney has a wealth of Neolithic sites to visit, of which Maeshowe, the Standing Stones of Stenness, the Ring of Brodgar and Skara Brae are the most spectacular. The great chambered cairn of Maeshowe is the largest and grandest of its type and dates from about 2750BC, while the Standing Stones and the Ring of Brodgar were erected at about the same time.

Maeshowe entrance passage lit up by the winter solstice sunset

All three monuments are situated in the heart of the West Mainland, surrounded by farmland and near the lochs of Stenness and Harray, in turn ringed by heather-covered low hills. There is a timeless and spacious feel to this landscape as a result of the dramatic confluence of sky, water and land.

The Standing Stones of Stenness date from about 3000BC

The Neolithic village of Skara Brae lies on the shore of the Bay of Skaill, and its well-preserved 5,000 year-old houses give a very good impression of life then. All four monuments form a World Heritage Site.

There is a Visitor Centre at Skara Brae with a museum, replica house and a shop, while at Tormiston Mill, next to Maeshowe, there is a shop and interpretative display.

The Ring of Brodgar is a spectacular henge monument over 100m across

Skara Brae Neolithic village was discovered after a storm in 1850

There are many other fascinating monuments and sites of interest ranging from the Neolithic to the 20th century which can be visited all over Orkney. Every parish and island has something different and special left by the people who inhabited the countryside during the last six millennia.

The Brough of Birsay is a tidal island off the north-west of the Mainland, and is the site of both Pictish and Viking settlements, with secular and monastic remains. In the nearby village of The Palace, the ruins of the 16th century Earl's Palace provide a gaunt reminder of the more recent past, while St Magnus Kirk is built on the site of a much older church.

Brough of Birsay aerial view showing Viking Age settlement ruins

The continuity of settlement in Orkney is well demonstrated by the Broch of Gurness, which is one of the best examples of over a possible 100 such structures in Orkney. It dates from the late Iron Age, the last centuries BC. The site was occupied for hundreds of years at least until early Norse times.

Broch of Gurness aerial view showing the broch and settlement

The 12th century St Magnus Cathedral in Kirkwall was built by the Norse Earl Rognvald Kolson in honour of his murdered uncle, Earl Magnus Erlendson. It dominates the town, and its warm-coloured Old Red Sandstone, unmarked by air pollution, makes the building especially attractive. The interior is particularly impressive and well-proportioned.

St Magnus Cathedral dates from 1137

The Italian Chapel was built during WW2 by Italian POWs

During WW2 several hundred Italian prisoners-of-war worked on the construction of the Churchill Barriers which were built to defend the eastern approaches of Scapa Flow. They built the Italian Chapel in their camp on Lamb Holm. This unusual and charming artefact of war survives now as a symbol of hope and peace.

NATURE AND ENVIRONMENT

As well as the huge array of ancient and more recent monuments, Orkney also has a rich and interesting natural environment. The combination of fertile farmland with the various other habitats makes it a very good place for wildlife, and especially birds. There are cliffs, marshes, moors and maritime heath as well as sheltered bays, small islands and lochs, all of which attract a variety of different species, depending on the season and weather.

Rough seas breaking over the cliffs of Yesnaby

The many superb beaches and dramatic cliffs also provide wonderful opportunities for walking. Whether just a stroll along the Bay of Skaill or Aikerness after visiting Skara Brae or the Broch of Gurness, or one of the many more adventurous walks, Orkney will never fail to please. The islands are also great for cycling, as the hills are not steep, and the roads quiet.

The Old Man of Hoy is one of Orkney's "trade marks"

The predominant daytime colours in Orkney are the greens, blues and browns of grass, water and moor. These colours vary with the season and are particularly vibrant in summer, but more muted in other seasons. Orkney is also famous for its sunsets and for its long hours of daylight in summer. The Northern Lights are occasionally seen, usually on a dark moonless winter night.

There are many superb beaches in Orkney, like Grobust on Westray

Aikerness beach in Evie overlooks Eynhallow Sound

The Orkney climate is much influenced by the sea, which varies in temperature by only a few degrees over the year. This ensures that winters are mild, but also that summers are never hot.

The weather is very variable, and it is possible to have every season in a day! The combination of constantly changing weather and changes in day length make for a huge variety of lighting conditions which makes Orkney a paradise for artists, photographers and lovers of the landscape in all seasons. Thus there is no "best" time to visit.

Orkney is famous for its marvellous summer light - 01:00 from Wideford Hill

There are many good locations for observing wildlife, including several RSPB Reserves. During the summer many thousands of birds breed in Orkney, and the cliff colonies of seabirds are especially impressive at Marwick Head in Birsay, and Noup Head on Westray. Both Grey and Common Seals also breed here.

Greens, blues and browns at the Loch of Stenness

Maritime Heath, for example, on Papay and on Rousay is a favourite nesting site for Terns and Arctic Skuas, while the Heather Moorland on the hills is home to Hen Harriers, Merlin and Short-eared Owls as well as many species of Waders. Curlews and Oystercatchers are particularly abundant.

Puffins are one of the many bird species which can be seen in Orkney

Orkney is also a good place to see migrants and winter visitors such as Great Northern Divers, Long-tailed Ducks, Goldeneye, Iceland Gulls and other species. The harbours at Kirkwall and Stromness are both good places to look for winter visitors, while the lochs in the vicinity of the Standing Stones are excellent places to see wildfowl in all seasons.

Orkney is home to a large number of Grey and Common Seals

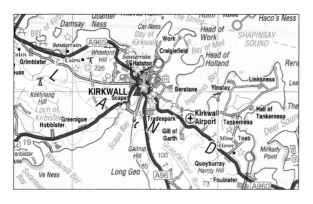

Kirkwall (ON *Kirkjuvagr - Church Bay*), as the main town in Orkney, makes a good starting point for a visit to the islands. It is first mentioned in the sagas as the dwelling place of Earl Rognvald Brusison about 1035, who built a church dedicated to King Olav of Norway there. The town developed around the Cathedral, and became the administrative and commercial centre, with its access to the North Isles, central position and sheltered harbour in the then much bigger Peedie Sea.

Today the winding main Street still follows the shape of the original settlement, and many of the fine old houses with end-on gables date from the 16th to 18th centuries. Narrow lanes run off the Street which has many attractive shops. At Broad Street it opens into the expanse of the grass-covered Kirk Green in front of St Magnus Cathedral.

The attractive harbour front is the scene of much activity with ferries and fishing boats. Over the last 200 years the pier has greatly expanded, but the Harbour

Basin still retains much of its charm.

The **Orkney Museum** is housed in Tankerness House, parts of which date from the 15th century. This museum is a good starting point from which to gain an insight into Orkney's rich past. The Tankerness House Gardens behind the museum make a pleasant place for a seat on a nice day. St Magnus Cathedral is across the road, and makes an excellent finale to a visit, with its peaceful interior.

The nearby **Bishop's** and **Earl's Palaces** date from Norse and Scottish times. The former was first built at the same time as the Cathedral, and was where King Haakon Haakonson died in 1263 after the "Battle" of Largs. The *"Moosie Tower"* was built during the 16th century.

The Earl's Palace was built by the notorious Earl Patrick

The Earl's Palace was built about 1600

Bishop's Palace - "Moosie" Tower

Kirkwall is dominated by the 12th century St Magnus Cathedral

Stewart in the early 17th century, but was only briefly occupied and was roofless by 1750. Patrick was executed for treason in 1615 and so had little time to enjoy his palace.

A very good vantage point from which to gain an overall impression of Orkney is from the top of **Wideford Hill**, just to the west of Kirkwall on the Old Finstown Road. It can be reached by footpath and by road. From the summit most of the North and South Isles, East and West Mainland and Scapa Flow can be seen.

Kirkwall is an excellent place to seek out interesting souvenirs or presents, with its wide variety of quality shops stocking knitwear, Orkney jewellery and crafts, local books, as well as many other home-produced items. In addition there is a good selection of Orkney food and drink products such as Highland Park Whisky, Orkney Herring, Orkney Cheese, smoked fish of various kinds and of course the famous Orkney Beef.

The **Highland Park Visitor Centre** on the edge of the town offers visits to the distillery and an excellent audiovisual introduction to Orkney and the making of Highland Park, as well as an enchanting shop which stocks many interesting items.

The ancient **St Magnus Cathedral** remains a symbol of the 600-year Norse sway over Orkney, and of the power and wealth of the Norse Earldom. For over 870 years it has dominated Kirkwall.

The Kirk Green and Broad Street

St Magnus Cathedral from the south-east

Haakon was succeeded by his son Paul, who was deposed in 1135 by Magnus' nephew Rognvald Kolson. Rognvald had vowed to build *"a stone minster at Kirkwall, and to dedicate it to Earl Magnus the Holy"*. In 1137 on St Lucia's Day (13th December) he is said to have laid the foundation stone.

Much of the finance came from local farmers under pressure from the Earl, and Durham masons were drafted in to supervise proceedings. The church was consecrated about 1150 when Magnus' remains were transferred from St Olaf's Kirk to a shrine in the east end of the building.

The choir was lengthened in the 13th century, and the nave extended also so that by the 14th century the Cathedral was more or less complete. Over the centuries it was allowed to fall into disrepair, but extensive restoration works have been carried out since the late 19th century. This work continues today.

St Magnus is built from Old Red Sandstone, said to have

In 1103 the cousins Magnus Erlendson and Haakon Paulson succeeded to the Earldom. At first all went well, but by about 1116 disputes had arisen, and it was agreed to meet on Egilsay on 16th April.

The agreement was that each Earl was to take only two ships, but Haakon arrived with eight and in uncompromising mood. Eventually his cook, Lifolf, was ordered to kill Magnus, which he did by cleaving his skull. A **ceno-**taph now stands on the spot where this act is said to have taken place and the roofless **St Magnus Church** on Egilsay is one of many churches named after the martyred Earl. Magnus was buried at Christ's Church at Birsay, and soon prayers were being said to him, with miraculous cures said to be taking place. Soon after Haakon made a pilgrimage to Rome, and on his return had the now ruined **St Nicholas Round Church** built at the Bu in Orphir, in about 1122.

St Nicholas Round Kirk, Orphir

St Magnus Church, Egilsay

been quarried at nearby Head of Holland, and also on Eday, lending the slightly austere exterior a warm look, which is particularly apparent in early morning or evening light.

The interior of the Cathedral is about 69m long and 30m across the transepts, while only 5m separates the pillars in the nave. Despite this, the overall impression is of space and balance with the attractive colours of the stone giving a very welcoming feel.

The Cathedral belongs to the people of Kirkwall and Orkney, having been largely financed by them over the centuries. The new St Magnus Centre, opened in 2001, is continued evidence of the strong role that the St Magnus Cathedral continues to play in Orkney society.

St Magnus stained glass window

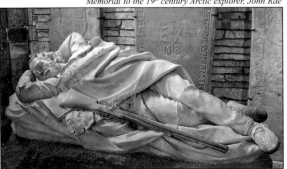

St Magnus Cathedral nave from the west door

West nave stained glass window

Memorial to the 19th century Arctic explorer, John Rae

Cenotaph on Egilsay

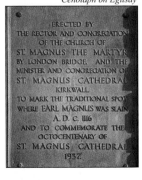

ERECTED BY
THE RECTOR AND CONGREGATION
OF THE CHURCH OF
ST. MAGNUS THE MARTYR
BY LONDON BRIDGE, AND THE
MINISTER AND CONGREGATION OF
ST. MAGNUS CATHEDRAL
KIRKWALL
TO MARK THE TRADITIONAL SPOT
WHERE EARL MAGNUS WAS SLAIN
A. D. c. 1116
AND TO COMMEMORATE THE
OCTOCENTENARY OF
ST. MAGNUS CATHEDRAL
1937

Highland Park Distillery

1 - Maltings - after steeping the barley, it is spread out on the malting floor and allowed to germinate

2- Loading the Kiln - the ? the kiln where it is dried ov

6 - Bonded Warehouse - the distillate is placed in sherry casks and laid down to mature for up to 25 years

5 - Still Room - when ferm distilled twice in the famili

The Highland Park Distillery, the most northerly in Scotland, was founded in 1798, on the site of a house which belonged to Magnus Eunson, a smuggler and illicit distiller, but also a Church Officer. On hearing that the Excisemen were after him, he removed all his casks from the kirk to his house, covered them with a coffin lid and a white cloth and called the congregation together around the whisky. When the customs arrived he was apparently conducting a funeral service, and a whispered "smallpox!" sent them off rapidly.

The site was chosen on account of the water supply which comes from springs in a small field called "Highland Park". The distillery

...barley is then placed in ...eat fire

3 - The Kiln - drying the malted barley - *the peat smoke imparts a rich aroma to the malt*

...on is complete the result is ... stills.

4 - Tun Room - *the milled malt is fermented in the mash tuns, and sampled at regular intervals*

has been owned by several people, having been founded by a David Robertson. It was even owned by a minister of the United Presbyterian Church for a time! The Grant family of Elgin first became associated with the distillery in 1888, finally selling to the Highland Distilleries Co. in 1936, which in turn was taken over by the Edrington Group in 1999.

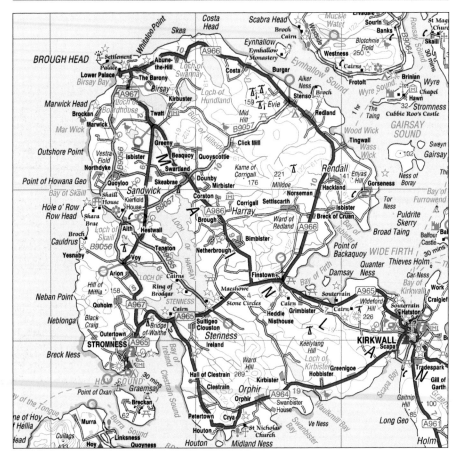

The West Mainland includes "The Heart of Neolithic Orkney", which is a designated World Heritage Site, including Maeshowe, the Standing Stones of Stenness, the Ring of Brodgar and Skara Brae, as well as parts of the surrounding area.

There is a strong argument for the whole of Orkney to be a World Heritage Site in view of its unique natural and cultural heritage. The West Mainland encompasses in a small and accessible area most of what is best about the archipelago.

The many sites of interest include dramatic coastline such as at Yesnaby, Marwick Head and the Brough of Birsay as well as fine beaches like Warebeth, the Bay of Skaill, Birsay, Aikerness or Waulkmill.

For birdwatchers and botanists, the huge variety of

"Grooved Ware" pottery

Ancient fossils at Yesnaby

Aerial view of the heart of Orkney

habitats ensures a wide range of species to see at any season, while anglers have a choice of several lochs on which to try their skills and luck. Walkers will also find a diverse selection of interesting routes, coastal or inland, easy or more strenuous.

Apart from the main four archaeological sites, there are many others dating from the Neolithic to the 20th century. These include Unstan, Cuween and Wideford Hill cairns, the Broch of Gurness and many more ruinous brochs as well as Pictish and Norse remains on the Brough of Birsay.

The Farm Museums at Corrigall and Kirbuster, the Click Mill and Boardhouse Mill, along with Skaill House, provide an insight into more recent times. Stromness Museum is also well worth a visit to see its wide-ranging and interesting displays.

Yesnaby Castle

NEOLITHIC ORKNEY - SKARA BRAE

Hut 1 with its stone dresser, beds, central fireplace and sea view

The 5,000 year-old Neolithic village of **Skara Brae** was buried under sand dunes at the Bay of Skaill, in the West Mainland, until 1850, when it was revealed by a big storm. The houses are so intact that it is easy to imagine their inhabitants going about their lives. The site was occupied sequentially from about 3100BC to about 2600BC, and consists of at least six houses, all joined together by a "street" and buried in a mound of midden except for the free-standing "workshop".

The houses are well con-structed with drains, (per-haps) damp-proof courses, stone dressers, beds, cup-boards and tanks. There are even cells with drains which might be toilets. All are quite similar in design and vary from about 6m x 6m to 4m x 4m. The roofs may have been supported by whalebone or driftwood couples and covered with hides and turf, perhaps with straw thatch, all held down with heather or straw ropes.

Panoramic view of Skara Brae with the Bay of Skaill in the background

Hut 8 appears to have been the workshop, with evidence of stone working, and pottery making. "Grooved Ware" pottery was found along with many bone and stone tools as well as jewellery items made from bone and shells.

The people were stock farmers and reared cattle, sheep, some pigs and deer and fished in the nearby sea, which would have been prolific with Cod, Haddock, Saithe and many species of shellfish at that time. They also grew Bere Barley.

Due to the small amount of flint in Orkney, chert was used to make cutting tools. Bone was much used, but wood was not well preserved, though presumably it would also have been extensively used.

Although no evidence of textile making was found, many tools which might have been used in working leather were found, suggesting that the people may have

Aerial view of Skara Brae

Hut 7 - now not visible to the public

been quite well dressed, perhaps using skins and furs rather than wool.

Skara Brae is contemporary with the other Orkney Neolithic monuments, but is so far the only well-preserved village to have been found and which can be visited, apart from the houses at Knap of Howar on Papa Westray and the settlement at Barnhouse in Stenness. The fact that it is so impressively designed and built suggests that its inhabitants were well settled in Orkney and not newcomers.

The "Street"

Maeshowe and Chambered Cairns

Winter sunset down the passage on 12th January - www.maeshowe.co.uk

the entrance passage aligned such that the setting sun illuminates the chamber for several weeks before and after the winter solstice.

Very few artefacts were found when the mound was cleared out in 1862, but the discovery of a large number of 12th century Norse runic inscriptions and other carvings somewhat mitigated this. These runes were carved about 1153 by Norsemen returning from the crusades and are of the form *"Ingibiorg, the fair widow..."* or *"Thorfinn carved these runes"*.

The chamber measures 4.5m square, similar to the smaller houses at Skara Brae, while the passage is 14.5m long and 1.4m high, and lined with very large stone slabs. The three chambers are each roofed with a single slab. The mound is surrounded by a ditch also dating from about 2750BC, but the bank seems to be more recent.

There are several other **Maeshowe-Type** chambered cairns to visit in

Maeshowe, or *Orkahaugr* in the Norse sagas, is one of the finest of all chambered cairns, of which there are many in Orkney. These tombs were built by Neolithic people from around 3200BC and were often used over a long period. Maeshowe dates from around 2750BC and is the largest and most splendid of its type to Orkney.

The stonework is engineered with great skill, with massive stone slabs which have been expertly cut and positioned. Also the mound has been carefully situated and

"Ingibiorg" runes carved by 12th century Vikings

Orkney including those at **Cuween Hill** near Finstown, on **Wideford Hill** near Kirkwall, and at **Quoyness** in Sanday. The other type is referred to as the **Orkney-Cromarty** group, which have upright "stalls", shelves at one or both ends and corbelled roofs. They may also have cells leading off the main chamber at floor level. Examples include **Unstan** in Stenness, the **Tomb of the Eagles** on South Ronaldsay as well as several on **Rousay**.

Excavation of a few of these cairns has yielded the remains of large numbers of people, and provided much information on lifestyle, life expectancy and diseases suffered as well as artefacts such as pottery and tools. Two types of pottery have been found - *"Grooved Ware"* and *"Unstan Ware".*

Some of the tombs seem to have been associated with a particular animal, such as Sea Eagles at the

Maeshowe from the north-east

eponomous Tomb of the Eagles, and dogs at Cuween. The Neolithic people went to great lengths to provide *"houses for the dead"* and clearly their ancestors were very important to them. The cairns may well have been used for rituals as well as burial.

Maeshowe sunset

Maeshowe interior showing cell, pillars and construction

The Maeshowe "dragon"

Maeshowe aerial view from the south-west

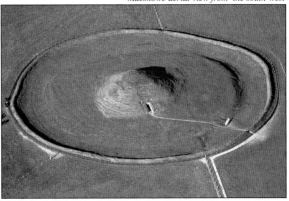

THE RING OF BRODGAR

Ring of Brodgar - aerial view from the north-west

The **Ring of Brodgar** (ON *Bruar-gardr*, Bridge Farm) is situated on a peninsula between the Lochs of Harray and Stenness, in the heart of the West Mainland. This very fine stone circle originally comprised 60 megaliths, of which 27 remain upright. It is a perfect circle, 103.7m in diameter and is surrounded by a rock-cut ditch 10m across and over 3m deep.

Dating from the same Neolithic period as Maeshowe and Skara Brae, the construction of the henge and ditch would have taken a lot of labour, implying an organised society with spare resources and some kind of strong beliefs. As with Maeshowe, the monument has been carefully situated, with clear views in all directions.

The monoliths resemble the uprights within Maeshowe in size and shape, ranging from about 2m to 4.5m in height, and often with angular faces or notches on one side. They are all aligned with their flat sides facing into the centre of the circle.

There is an outlying standing stone, the **Comet Stone**, to the south east as well as several mounds nearby

Ring of Brodgar - panoramic view from the centre of the ring - looking towards Harray Loch

which could date from the Bronze Age. They may be points for viewing the variety of solar alignments relating to the solstices, equinoxes, Beltane and other dates which have been observed or suggested.

This may have been the intention of the designer or not, but will always remain enigmatic. Alignments with lunar phenomena have also been observed and suggested, particularly at the times of major lunar standstills, every 18.6 years.

Nowhere does the feeling of space, where water, land and sky all seem to merge feel stronger than at Brodgar. The constantly changing Orkney light and weather mean that the site can be visited at any season or time of day and always look different. Although we know nothing about the beliefs of the Neolithic people who built the Ring of Brodgar it is clear that they were a highly motivated and imaginative society.

Ring of Brodgar - summer sunset

The Ring of Brodgar takes on a pristine appearance in the snow

THE STANDING STONES OF STENNESS

Standing Stones of Stenness - midsummer sunset

The **Standing Stones of Stenness** originally comprised of a circle of perhaps 12 monoliths, surrounded by a ditch 2m deep, 7m wide and 44m in diameter. The tallest stone is over 5m high. In addition there is a hearth-like stone setting in the centre. The site dates from about 3000BC and is thus older than Maeshowe or Brodgar.

Holes for more stones or wooden uprights were also discovered within the circle

Hoy Hills and Loch of Stenness - midwinter sunset with "flashing" sun

and nearby, suggesting that the site was originally more complex.

The nearby **Watchstone** stands at the side of the Loch of Stenness. Observed from here some days before and after the winter solstice, the sun disappears behind the Ward Hill of Hoy, and then reappears momentarily before finally setting.

There are several other standing stones in the vicinity, the **Barnhouse Stone** near the main road, and a pair of smaller monoliths on the north side of the Brodgar Bridge. In addition there used to be the **Stone of Odin**, which was destroyed in 1814.

Watchstone - midsummer sunset

The Stone of Odin

This stone was broken up and used to build a shed, but was a famous landmark. It had a hole through which lovers and others could hold hands and thus seal their vows. The *Oath of Odin* was binding on any contract, and also credited with healing powers.

Nearby is the **Neolithic Village of Barnhouse** on the edge of the Loch of Harray. The bases of at least 15 free-standing houses are indicated here, each with a central hearth, and beds similar to those at Skara Brae. Two were bigger than the rest, the largest being 7m square internally with 3m thick walls. At midsummer the setting sun shines directly down the entrance passage of this house.

This structure resembles some of the chambered cairns, especially Maeshowe, and may have been a meeting-hall associated with events at the Standing Stones. Flint and other stone tools were found as well as

Grooved Ware pottery, similar to that from Skara Brae and the Standing Stones.

Of the two types of pottery associated with the Orkney

Unstan Ware bowls

archaeological sites, Unstan Ware seems to be the older, but it is not clear whether the two designs are due to date, fashion, social group, or manufacture method.

Pottery decoration

Barnhouse Neolithic village - large house entrance

THE BROUGH OF BIRSAY

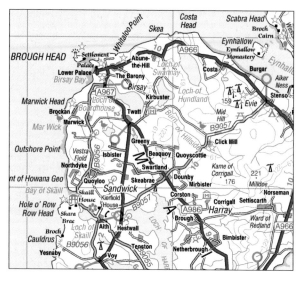

Near the church lies an extensive area of buildings - complete with bath-house and under floor central heating. It is thought that Earl Thorfinn the Mighty's 11th century cathedral and palace were in the village, which is called "The Palace".

On the Point of Buckquoy a number of figure-of-eight shaped Pictish houses of similar age to the one at Gurness have been excavated, but none are on display. However "Groatie Buckies" (Cowrie Shells) may be found on the beach here in compensation.

The Brough of Birsay is a tidal island off the northwest corner of the Mainland. There are remains of a large Viking settlement, which is underlain by Pictish buildings. Bronze casting was important in Pictish times and a large symbol stone was also found. Settlement seems to have started about the 6th century AD.

Most of the ruins visible today are Viking, the small church is 12th century, but there may be an earlier Celtic one below it. On the slopes above the church are the outlines of several Norse longhouses up to 20m long, together with outhouses, which can be clearly seen from the air.

Apart from the ancient monuments, the Brough has a lighthouse dating from 1925, and the whole area is a very pleasant place for a walk or to watch rough seas from the shelter of the car during a winter storm. It is also possible to see Puffins here during the breeding season.

Brough of Birsay from the south with a rough sea

Replica of Pictish symbol stone

The **Earl's Palace** at "The Palace" village was built by Earl Robert Stewart in the late 16th century and consists of four wings surrounding a large courtyard which has a well in the middle. It was said to be *"a sumptuous and stately mansion"* in 1633. Stewart was a half-brother of Mary Queen of Scots.

The large exposed bay to the east of the Brough is called **Skipi Geo**. There is a fine walk from the car park to the Whale Bone, from where there are spectacular views on rough days. In summer the whole area is awash with wild flowers, including Thrift, spring Squill, Grass of Parnassus and Sea Plantain.

One of the last working examples of a 19th century mill, **Barony Water Mill** is open to the public and is in working order. Beremeal can still be made here, being ground from the old-fashioned four-row barley which is still grown in Orkney and which was formerly used to make ale and, later, whisky.

Marwick Head (87m) lies to the south of the village, and is an RSPB Reserve. In early summer it teems with breeding seabirds and is a very good place to view Guillemots, Razorbills, Fulmars, Kittiwakes, Rock Doves, Puffins, and even perhaps a Peregrine. The clifftops are carpeted by a profusion of Thrift and other

The Earl's Palace dates from the late 16th century

Skipi Geo and the Whalebone on a rough day

Brough of Birsay aerial view showing Viking Age ruins

Marwick Head from the north

Kitchener Memorial, Birsay

wild flowers and yellow lichens in summer, which adds to the wild beauty of the cliffs.

The Old Red Sandstone rock has level beds and weathers into a myriad of small ledges which are ideal for nesting seabirds. There are also plentiful food supplies in the neighbouring waters.

There are several other **RSPB Reserves** in the West Mainland. These include the Loons, near Marwick Head, the Birsay Moors and Hobbister in Orphir. Other good places for birds are the Loch of Harray, Burgar Hill in Evie and the harbours of Kirkwall and Stromness.

The tower at the highest point of Marwick Head was erected after WW1 to commemorate the Minister of War, Kitchener, and the crew of *HMS Hampshire,* which was sunk here in 1916, probably by a mine. The cruiser was taking Kitchener to Russia when the sinking happened. There were very few survivors.

Further south along the west coast of the Mainland lies the **Bay of Skaill**, with its famous Neolithic village of Skara Brae. A stroll here is much recommended at any season, whether benign on a summer's day or wild in a winter storm.

The **Head O'Row** is on the south side of the bay and has superb views to north and south as well as a blow hole, the **Hole O'Row**, through which waves explode on a rough day. There is superb clifftop walk from Skaill to **Yesnaby**, with its the wild cliff scenery. During a storm huge waves crash into and over the cliffs. The **Castle of Yesnaby** is a mini version of the Old Man of Hoy, which can be seen from here.

Stromatolites, fossils which date from about 350 million years ago, may be seen here. Yesnaby is also one of the best places to see the rare **Primula scotica**, which flowers in May and July and

Bay of Skaill and Skara Brae

Primula scotica

Aerial view of the Brough of Bigging, Yesnaby, Sandwick

can be spotted from the approach road. This hardy little plant only grows in Orkney and the north coast of Scotland. It has small magenta flowers.

In summer Spring Squill, Thrift, Grass of Parnassus and Sea Plantain give the maritime heath a warm glow. Yesnaby has many characters depending on the season, time of day and weather.

Hoy Sound from Orphir

Yesnaby Castle with Thrift

Orphir, on the south coast of the West Mainland is a complete contrast to the west coast, with peaceful views over Hoy and Scapa Flow. Swanbister Bay and Waulkmill Bay have attractive beaches while the Ward Hill (268m) is the highest on the Mainland.

The Round Kirk was built by Haakon Paulson about 1122, perhaps in atonement for the murder of his cousin, Earl Magnus. The nearby Orkneyinga Saga Centre tells the story of the Earls.

THE BROCH OF GURNESS, EVIE

The Broch of Gurness with surrounding settlement ditches and ramparts

Brochs (ON *Borg*, stronghold) are unique to Scotland and Orkney has about 100. They developed from roundhouses which first appeared around 700BC. Brochs typically have a large tower, up to 20m in diameter with hollow walls up to 5m thick at the base. The walls have an internal staircase and the structures could be up to 15m tall. Most brochs are sited on or near the coast, but there a number in the West Mainland that are inland.

The **Broch of Gurness at Aikerness in Evie,** remains an imposing building with its ramparts and ditches, broch tower and extensive surrounding settlement. The site was occupied from the Iron Age through Pictish and into Norse times.

The broch was surrounded by three massive ramparts and deep ditches, and may well have had a tall tower. Inside there is a central hearth and quite an elaborate

underground well with a collecting tank. The space between the broch and the ramparts encloses a small village which could have been occupied by 30 or so families.

The houses share walls and are furnished in stone with hearths, cooking tanks, drains, box beds, storage cupboards and even a toilet.

During excavation many artefacts were found, includ-

The Broch of Gurness from the entrance on the east side

The Broch of Gurness from the west with surrounding ditches and ramparts

ing fragments of Roman amphorae from about 100AD, Pictish Ogam inscriptions and other Pictish artefacts as well as a 9th century Viking female burial.

Also at Gurness is the only example of shamrock-shaped multicellular Pictish houses currently on view in Orkney. These were rebuilt near the entrance as originally they were built into the broch mound. The small museum has a shop, and an excellent interpretation area.

Aikerness has a fine beach and is a good place to see seals, Otters and seabirds. The links and roadside verges are also very good for wild flowers in summer.

Other good brochs to visit include Midhowe on Rousay, Burgar in Sandwick, Dingieshowe in Deerness, Burrian on North Ronaldsay and Burroughstone on Shapinsay.

Earthhouses Another interesting development starting in about 600BC is the Earthhouse or souterrain. Typical examples at Rennibister in Firth and Grain near Kirkwall can be visited.

These underground structures are thought to be cellars from long-gone roundhouses. They were probably used for storage, and any resemblance to chambered cairns is most likely superficial.

Pictish houses at Gurness

Rennibister Earthhouse

SKAILL HOUSE, SANDWICK

Skaill House from the west

Skaill House is situated near Skara Brae on the west coast of the Mainland. It is one of a small number of mansion houses in Orkney which are open to the public as museums, and dates partly from the 17th century, when part of the Earldom estate passed to the Bishopric under Bishop Graham in 1615.

This Bishop proceeded to "acquire" a substantial amount of land from bishopric property and smallholdings, in the name of his eldest son, John, who became the first Laird. The present Laird, Major Malcolm Macrae, is the 12th and he has renovated the property as a museum.

The oldest part of the house was built by Bishop Graham in the 1620's and much of the house dates from the 18th century, with further additions over the next two centuries.

The tour is a good insight to the lives of the Lairds and their families, with connections to many historic events and characters. These include some of Captain Cook's dinner service, a cupboard called the Armada Chest, with panels said to have come from a Spanish ship in 1588 and one of Bishop Graham's beds.

The house allegedly is haunted, and during renovation work 15 skeletons were found near the east porch, which are thought to be early Christian.

There is a gift shop and the property is open from April to September. A visit makes an interesting contrast to Skara Brae.

Other mansion houses which may be visited include Balfour Castle on Shapinsay, Carrick House on Eday and Melsetter House on Hoy, all by arrangement..

Dining Room

Bishop Graham's bed

The two Farm Museums, at **Kirbuster** in Birsay and **Corrigall** in Harray, are in strong contrast to Skaill House and represent examples of ordinary houses from the early and late 19th century respectively. Both have a dwelling house, byre, barn, corn drying kiln and outhouses.

Kirbuster Museum showing fireback

Kirbuster Farm has no chimney, but instead an open fire with a *"fireback"* and a wooden smoke-hole in the roof with *"skylin"*. The smoke-hole also served to let extra light in. There is a neuk bed, reminiscent of the beds at Skara Brae built into one wall. Despite the lack of a chimney the house is not very smoky inside.

Corrigall Farm is more modern with chimneys and a higher roof but is otherwise similar. The bedroom end has boxbeds, and the floors are all of flagstone. On display are a variety of old implements, traditional crafts, furnishings and tools, as well as a variety of livestock.

Corrigall Farm Museum

The Click Mill

The **Click Mill** near Dounby is a late 19th century example of a so-called "Norse" vertical axis corn mill. Named because of the noise made during operation, these were basically mechanised quernstones, and were common from Norse and possibly earlier times until the later 19th century when larger water mills became popular.

STROMNESS

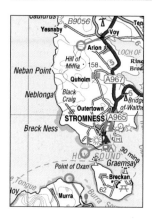

Stromness from the Ness

Stromness (ON *Straum-nes*, Stream Point) was also called *Hamnavoe* (Harbour Bay) by the Vikings. This excellent harbour is the ferry terminal for the crossing to Scrabster in Caithness. There are also many small fishing boats and dive boats which work from here, and one of Orkney's three RNLI Lifeboats is based here.

The town dates from the 17th century and for many years supplied water, stores and crewmen to ships taking the northern route around Britain as well as ships of the Hudson's Bay Company and whalers. During the Herring Boom in the late 19th and early 20th centuries it was also very busy.

The winding, flagstone-paved street is the backbone of the town. Many of the houses on the shore side have their own piers, while the houses higher up are reached by a multitude of narrow lanes. The lack of

space for new development in the town has ensured that it has retained its attractive character, with the industrial area being situated on the outskirts.

The intimate nature of the town makes Stromness popular with visitors and several events take place here including the Orkney Traditional Folk Festival, the Stromness Shopping Week and the Beer Festival.

The **Stromness Museum** has a fascinating series of displays on mostly maritime and natural history themes.

Stromness - houses and piers

Stromness - panoramic view from the ferry showing the characteristic shore front houses with end-on gables and piers

Stromness - sunset from Cairston Road

These include the Hudson's Bay Company connection, the scuttle of the WW1 German High Seas Fleet, and Orkney birds, mammals, molluscs and insects.

Also well worth a visit is the **Pier Arts Centre** with its permanent collection of 20th century art and temporary exhibitions. This attractive old building was once the agency and store for the Hudson's Bay Company and is built on a pier near the ferry terminal. It has recently been refurbished and extended to accommodate a greater variety of work.

There are many interesting shops in Stromness, offering a range of local crafts, knitwear, books and art, as well as several grocers and hardware shops.. Parking is not very practical in the narrow street but there are plenty of spaces on the approach road.

Apart from the timeless attraction of watching boats and people around the harbour, Stromness has a golf course and a variety of fine walks. There is an excellent panoramic view from **Brinkie's Brae** (94m) above the town.

The beach of **Warebeth** lies to the west and offers fine views of the Hoy Hills and Hoy Sound. There is a fine coastal walk to it via the Point of Ness. This continues to Breckness. This shore has many interesting rock formations which date from 350 million years ago.

At the north end of Outertown, the **Black Craig** (111m) offers a fine panorama from the old coastguard hut. A little further on is North Gaulton Castle, a fine, but little visited, rock stack.

Stromness - Victoria Street

Warebeth beach with the Hoy Hills in the background

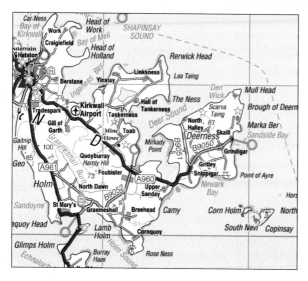

The **East Mainland** parishes of **Tankerness**, **Holm** and **Deerness** have much to offer the visitor, having a charm all of their own and being like a separate island in many ways. The area is generally low-lying and mostly farmland, but all the

same has much of interest to see and do including many fine beaches, some spectacular cliffs and good walking.

There is much evidence of early occupation in the form of burnt mounds and brochs, most

notably **Dingieshowe** on the Deerness isthmus. The only ancient monument open to the visitor is **Minehowe**. This enigmatic, well-like Iron Age structure has 29 stone steps which descend in two flights to a small chamber. Minehowe is a small part of a large unexplored prehistoric landscape.

There are many good birding sites here including the flat sands at **Mill Sands** and **St Peter's Pool**, in Tankerness, **St Mary's Loch** and **Graemeshall Loch**, in Holm, the Mull Head cliffs and moors, and the island of Copinsay. The latter is an RSPB Reserve and hard to reach, but well worth the effort.

Mull Head in Deerness is a Nature Reserve with indicated paths. Near the entrance the **Gloup** is a a large partially collapsed cave which can be entered from seaward. The deep chasm needs to be observed with care. The low cliffs at Mull Head are a good place to see seabirds and seals.

Sandside, **Newark** and **Dingieshowe** are all very fine beaches for a walk or picnic. Keep a good look out at Newark Bay in case you should see the mermaid! The **Covenanters' Memorial** on the north side of Deerness is a poignant reminder of the spot where about 250 political prisoners were drowned in 1688 whilst being transported to

Minehowe - an enigmatic Iron Age monument

The Gloup, a collapsed cave

Copinsay cliffs from the east

the West Indies aboard the "Crown". The Covenanters were against the imposition of the *Book of Common Prayer* by Charles II.

The pretty village of **St Mary's** in Holm overlooks **Holm Sound**, through which *U47* sailed in 1939 on its way to sink *HMS Royal Oak*. There is a good view of the sound and the Churchill Barriers from the hill east of the village.

Dingieshowe Broch Mound

The fertile area in the south east corner is known as **Paplay**, where the Vikings found a large monastic settlement. No archaeological remains have been excavated from this time here, but a high status Pictish farmstead at Skaill in Deerness was examined some time ago.

Holm Sound and Scapa Flow from Hurtiso

Although the East Mainland does not have the archaeology or spectacular coastal scenery of the West Mainland, it offers another appealing aspect of Orkney - almost like going to a different island without having to take a ferry.

Newark Bay, where mermaids are said to appear

Diver examines gun on WW2 German wreck "F2"

The wreck of *HMS Royal Oak* has recently been leaking considerable quantities of fuel oil and has become a pollution threat. As a result the Royal Navy is now removing the oil.

Scapa Flow was used as the main base of the British Home Fleet in both WW1 and WW2 due to it being a large land-locked harbour with deep entrances and deep water anchorages. In both wars it took some time to make it secure.

The harbour saw dramatic actions in both wars. After WW1 74 vessels of the **German High Seas Fleet** were interned here, and on 21st June 1919 they were nearly all scuttled. Some were beached, but most sank. The majority of the fleet was salvaged during the 1920s and 1930s, but three battleships and four cruisers remain and are much visited by scuba divers today.

In 1939 the U-boat *U47* crept into Scapa Flow through Holm Sound and torpedoed **HMS Royal Oak**, with the loss of 833 crew. This action was to result in the construction of the Churchill Barriers and a huge increase in the defences in general.

Up to 40,000 men were based in Orkney at the peak of activity in WW2, and once secured maximum advantage was taken of the strategically important position of Scapa Flow. Much evidence still remains of the defences - coastal batteries, searchlight emplacements, old airfields, and parts of the naval base at Lyness on Hoy, where the **Scapa Flow Visitor Centre**, based in an old pumphouse, is a museum and interpretation centre about Scapa Flow.

During WW2, aircraft carriers were very important and Orkney served as base for repairs and training for many of their aircraft. The action where *Bismarck* was sunk succeeded due to the seemingly archaic Fairey

Scapa Flow panoramic view from Glimps Holm

"SMS Hindenberg"

"SMS Derfflinger" sinking June 1919

Swordfish torpedo bombers which doggedly searched out the battleship and despite their apparent frailty damaged the ship's rudder.

"HMS Royal Oak" firing her main armament

In the 1970's oil was first exploited in the North Sea, and the **Flotta Oil Terminal** continues to process and export large quantities of crude. Oil is also handled from the fields to the west of Orkney by shuttle tanker.

Scapa Flow is winter home to many birds which breed in the Arctic, including Great Northern Divers and Long-tailed Ducks. It is occasionally visited by pods of young Sperm Whales and its shores are home to the elusive Otter.

Fairey "Swordfish" in flight

Flotta Oil Terminal

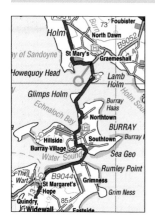

The Italian Chapel was built by Italian prisoners of war in WW2

The **Italian Chapel**, *"the Miracle of Camp 60"*, built by Italian Prisoners of War of Camp 60, who arrived in January 1942 to help build the Churchill Barriers, is an unusual memorial to the war.

To brighten up the cheerless camp of Nissen huts the Italians made paths and planted flowerbeds. Domenico Chiocchetti made the St George and the Dragon statue from barbed wire and cement, to preside over the camp square. The prisoners soon had a theatre and a recreational hut com-plete with a concrete billiard table, but they lacked a chapel.

In late 1943 two Nissen huts were joined end to end and Domenico Chiocchetti set to work, aided by a small num-ber of other POWs. One end was to be the Chapel, the other a school.

The hut was lined with plas-terboard and an altar with altar-rail cast in concrete. Chiocchetti painted the Madonna and Child behind the altar which is based on a 19th century painting by Nicolo Barabino inspired by a card his mother had given to him. He also frescoed a White Dove, the symbol of the Holy Spirit, at the centre of the vault and included the symbols of the four Evangelists around it, as well as two Cherubim and two Seraphim lower down.

The upper parts of the interi-or appear like brick with vaulting, while the lower walls are painted to look like carved marble. The "vaults" in the ceiling are especially well executed, and the visu-al effect is quite stunning. Palumbo, a metalworker, made candelabra and the

St George and the Dragon

The Italian Chapel with Holm Sound in the background

Head of Christ above the door

D Chiocchetti at work

rood screen and gates. A façade was erected with the help of Bruttapasta, with an archway and pillars. A belfry was mounted on top and a moulded head of Christ in red clay was placed on the front of the arch. The whole exterior of the hut was then covered with a thick coat of cement, never in short supply during the building of the Barriers!

Chiocchetti returned to Orkney in 1960, when he did much to restore the internal paintwork of the chapel. In 1961 his hometown, Moena, near Bolzano in the Dolomites, gifted a wayside shrine, a carved figure of Christ erected outside the Chapel, to the people of Orkney. More recently much exterior work has been done to restore and preserve the Chapel and the memorial statue for the future.

The Italian Chapel is now one of the most-visited monuments in Orkney and is a fitting memorial to those lost in wartime. Chiocchetti, in addressing the Orcadian people, said, *"The chapel is yours - for you to love and preserve. I take with me to Italy the remembrance of your kindness and wonderful hospitality. I shall remember you always, and my children shall learn from me to love you. I thank (you)....for having given me the joy of seeing again the little chapel of Lambholm where I, in leaving, leave a part of my heart.".*

It is somewhat ironic that most of the many visitors to Orkney cross the Churchill Barriers. They come not to remember the English war leader, or to marvel at military engineering, but to visit our little Italian shrine, which is a monument to hope and faith in exile.

The Italian Chapel interior

Aerial view of Barrier #1 after completion

Work in progress on Barrier #3

The tide was strong in Holm Sound

HMS "Royal Oak" at sea

Blockship "Reginald" off Barrier #3

The **Churchill Barriers** were ordered to be built by Churchill in 1940 after the sinking of *HMS Royal Oak* in 1939, by the German U-boat, *U47*. to seal off the eastern approaches to Scapa Flow. The Balfour Beatty firm was appointed as contractors and to solve the labour shortage, several hundred Italian prisoners-of-war were drafted in early 1942 to assist in the work.

Camps and works were set up in the east Mainland, and on Lamb Holm, Gimps Holm and Burray. Nearly 1 million cubic metres of rock in wire bolsters was used to complete the four Barriers, and by late 1942 they were breaking the surface. Over 50,000 5 and 10-ton concrete blocks were then used to clad the sides.

Today the Barriers provide Orkney's only fixed transport links between the mainland and other islands. Beaches have built up in Weddel and Water Sound on the east side of Barriers #3 and #4. Many overwintering species of birds, as well as occasional whales or dolphins can be seen from the Barriers.

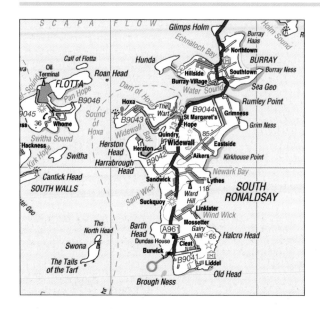

England, but "Hope" comes from ON *Hjop* (Bay), and not the English word "hope".

In the village are the **Old Smiddy Museum**, several interesting shops and craft workshops as well as the renowned Creel Restaurant. At Sand O'Right, the **Boys' Ploughing Match** is held each August. The girls dress up as horses and the boys as ploughmen. Rigs are worked in the sand using ploughs which have often been handed down over generations.

The Marine-Life Aquarium at Pool Farmhouse *"offers a unique chance to see and understand some aspects of the marine environment."*, while at the **Hoxa Tapestry Gallery**, Leila Thomson weaves wonderful tapestries *"inspired by the life and landscape of Orkney."*

The **Tomb of the Eagles** is at the south end, near Burwick. This Orkney-Cromarty type chambered cairn is only one of two which have been excavated recently, and strongly resembles Unstan Cairn in Stenness. The remains of about 340 individuals were found. Of particular interest was the discovery of skele-

South Ronaldsay and **Burray** are now joined to the Mainland by the **Churchill Barriers** and thus are easily accessed. There are many sites of interest apart from the Barriers, their associated blockships and the lovely sandy beaches which have built up at Barriers #3 and #4.

On **Burray** (ON *Borgarey*, Broch Island) the **Orkney Fossil and Heritage Centre** has displays of Orkney rocks and fossils and tells the story of Orkney's geology, as well as relics of bye-gone days. There is

a gift shop and tea room.which is open from April to October. The nearby Echnaloch is particularly good for wildfowl at all times of year. Many overwintering species can also be seen from the Barriers.

South Ronaldsay (ON *Rognvald's-ey*) has a special charm. The small village of St Margaret's Hope dates from the 17th and 18th centuries. The bay is said to be named after a 13th century Norse princess who died in 1290 while on her way to marry Prince Edward of

Fossil and Vintage Centre, Viewforth, Burray

Boys' Ploughing Match, South Ronaldsay

tons and talons of Sea Eagles - hence the name.

The cairn was built about 3150BC and used for up to 800 years. Over 40 broken Unstan Ware pots were found, as well as fish and animal bones and charred barley. Beautifully carved stone objects and rougher stone tools are on display along with some of the skulls in the museum where they can be examined closely. The human remains have revealed much about the lives of these people.

The nearby **Liddle Burnt Mound** dates from the Bronze Age, from perhaps 1000BC, and has a central trough which was used to cook joints of meat by throwing in stones heated in a fire - hence the mound of burnt stones.

John o'Groats Ferries runs throughout the summer between John o'Groats in Caithness and Burwick in around 45 minutes. **Pentland Ferries** also operate a daily ro-ro ferry between Gills Bay in Caithness and St. Margarets Hope, offering a scenic alternative to the route between Stromness and Scrabster.

Tomb of the Eagles, interior of the main chamber

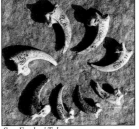

Sea Eagles' Talons

Skull from Tomb of the Eagles

Blockship "Collindoc" at Cara, South Ronaldsay (Barrier #4)

St Margaret's Hope, South Ronaldsay

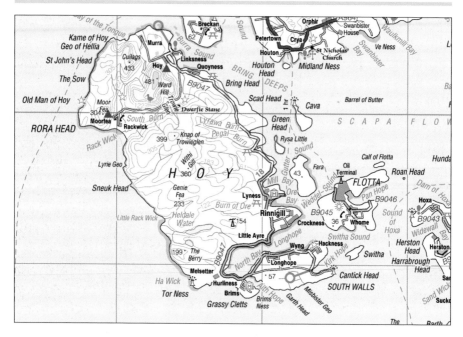

Hoy (ON *Ha-ey*, High Island) is the second largest of the Orkney Islands and different in character from the others. The north end is hilly with the **Ward Hill** (479m) and **Cuilags** (433m) being prominent landmarks from many parts of Orkney. Much of the north end of Hoy is an **RSPB Reserve**.

The north and west coasts have spectacular cliffs, only the south end being low and fertile. One of Orkney's most well-known icons is the famous rock stack, the **Old Man of Hoy** (137m), which stands on a lava platform. The ferry passes the Hoy cliffs on its way across the Pentland Firth, allowing a stunning view of the noble stack..

The wide sweep of **Rackwick,** on the north west side with a sand and boulder beach bounded on both sides by high cliffs, is well appreciated from the path to the Old Man, from which there are good views across the Pentland Firth to Scotland. Rackwick has a beauty and climate all of its own, but beware the midgies!.

Rackwick from the path to the Old Man of Hoy

The imposing craigs at **St John's Head** (351m) are the highest vertical sea .cliffs in Britain. The horizontal beds of sandstone have weathered to give dramatic reds and yellows, which are especially vibrant with a low evening sun.

Below the Ward Hill, on the road to Rackwick, lies the enigmatic **Dwarfie Stone** with

The Old Man of Hoy (137m) from the ferry

its hand-carved chamber. This may be Neolithic, but is unique as the only such tomb in UK. It must have taken a lot of work using only hand tools to excavate the cavity.

There are good views across Scapa Flow from the road along the east coast to **North and South Walls** (ON *Vagr*, Voe or Bay), where the landscape is more like the rest of Orkney. Most of the population lives at the south end of the island.

Near the Water of Hoy, a small fenced memorial to Betty Corrigall lies on the parish boundary. This young girl committed suicide in the 19th century after becoming pregnant to a local man who left on a whaling ship for the *Nor'Wast*.

Further south, **Pegal Burn** is the largest stream in Orkney. This attractive watercourse and estuary is a fine place for a picnic and also to see an Otter if you are lucky.

Lyness was a large naval base during both World Wars and was known as *HMS Prosperine*. Underground oil storage tanks, a large harbour, dubbed *"Golden Wharf"* on account of its cost, and a huge array of buildings sprang up. Now Most of this has now been removed, and Lyness is the ferry terminal for Houton on the Mainland and for Flotta.

Although most of the detritus of war has now been tidied up

Pegal Burn

The Dwarfie Stone

Hackness Martello Tower

the poignant **Naval Cemetery** remains as a reminder of the human sacrifice involved.

The **Naval HQ and Communications Centre** on the hill above has fine views. The **Scapa Flow Visitor Centre** is in what was the pumphouse serving the Royal Navy fuel oil tanks during WW2. One of the oil tanks has also been retained and contains displays of military equipment and artefacts.

Inside the pumphouse the machinery has been renovated and there are displays of small artefacts, photographs and

documents relating to the two World Wars. Outside several WW1 German guns, railway stock used in WW2 and a propeller off *HMS Hampshire* can be seen.

Melsetter House and Rysa Lodge were designed by William Lethaby in Arts and Crafts style for the Middlemore family. At Melsetter the original house dating from 1738 is part of the 1898 design, forming the most attractive country house in Orkney.

Longhope Lifeboat Station at Brims is now a museum

whose main exhibit is the lifeboat which served here 1933-1962, the *Thomas McCunn*. Since being established in 1874, many successful rescues were undertaken from here, and perhaps coxswain Dan Kirkpatrick wase most deserving of fame.

It was from here that he and his crew left in the lifeboat *TGB* to go to the aid of a Liberian freighter, Irene, in March 1969. Sadly all were lost in tumultuous seas in the Pentland Firth. A bronze statue in Osmondwall Cemetery honours the *TGB* crew.

The present Longhope Lifeboat, The Helen Comrie, is of the latest Tamar class, and was on station in October 2006. She is based in the little harbour at Longhope.

At **Hackness** there is a Martello Tower and gun battery, one of two built during the early 19th century Napoleonic Wars to protect shipping from marauding American privateers. Convoys were introduced at that time to guard merchant vessels from attack, and Longhope was a good place for ships to gather.

The towers had 24-pounder-guns mounted on top, while the nearby battery had eight 24-pounder guns, with barracks, stores and a magazine. The site is now managed by Historic Scotland, and has been extensively renovated.

Longhope Harbour

The Hoy Hills and Hoy Sound from the Point of Ness, Stromness

Cantick Head Lighthouse was completed in 1858 by David Stevenson. It was automated in 1991. There are good views over the Pentland Firth from here and Killer Whales have been seen close in at times.

In contrast to the dramatic cliffs of North Hoy, the low cliffs, fine beaches and fertile land make for much more gentle walking. *Primula scotica* and other maritime heath plants thrive along the south coast.

Nature Otters and seals live around the coasts and many of Orkney's characteristic birds thrive here. In winter North Bay is excellent for waders and wintering wildfowl, and a flock of Barnacle Geese stays here each winter.

Archaeology There are several broch mounds around Longhope, but perhaps the most interesting association dates from 995, when King Olaf Tryggvason of Norway forcibly converted Earl Sigurd the Stout to Christianity at Osmondwall on pain of killing Sigurd's son.

A trip to Hoy with its varied and dramatic scenery, wonderful views of the rest of Orkney and historic sites from the rel-

Longhope Lifeboat Memorial

atively recent past makes an interesting addition to any visit to Orkney. It can be reached from both Houton or Stromness by ferry, and accommodation is available.

Melsetter House

Cantick Head Lighthouse

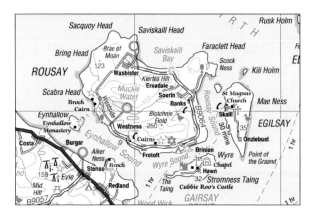

Rousay (ON *Hrolfs-ey* - Rolf's Island) has been called *"The Egypt of the North"* due to its concentration of prehistoric tombs and other monuments. This round, hilly island has a road around the coast and makes a pleasant excursion from the Mainland via the ro-ro ferry from Tingwall in Rendall.

Near the pier is the unusual two-tiered chambered cairn of **Taversoe Tuick**. This unique little tomb also has two entrances. Further west are two more chambered cairns at **Blackhammar** and **Yarso**. Both are of the "stalled" type and are divided up by upright slabs as in a byre.

Blackhammar only contained two burials and a broken Unstan Ware bowl, while Yarso had remains of at least 21 people. In both cases flint and bone tools were found as well as deer bones at Yarso.

Midhowe stalled cairn is the largest chambered cairn in Orkney. The chamber measures 23x4m and is divided by 12 pairs of "stalls". About 25 bodies had been laid in a crouched position on or under shelves between the stalls. The outside walls are carefully built with stones set at an angle like the designs on Unstan Ware pottery.

Midhowe forms part of the

Westness Walk, which also takes in the **Midhowe Broch**, whose walls still reach 4.3m in height. This Iron Age building was occupied from about 200BC to 200AD and finds included some Roman arte- such as including pottery and a bronze ladle. There was also evidence of bronze working including crucibles, moulds and jewellery.

On Moaness near Westness farm is the site of a Pictish and Viking cemetery. Many Viking brooches, pins, tools and weapons were found, including an elaborate Celtic brooch-pin. The boat graves contained the remains of two men buried with their weapons, one of whom had four arrowheads in his body.

Above the Bay of Swandro lie the ruins of a Norse Farm and nearby on Moaness there is a Norse boat shed and slipway. There is another broch at Swandro, while Skaill is an 18th century farm whose tenants were evicted by General Burroughs in the 19th century. Nearby St Mary's Kirk became disused in 1820. Thus the Westness area was the

Blackhammar chambered cairn

Yarso chambered cairn

Rousay aerial from the north west, Egilsay and Wyre are in the background and Eynhallow is on the right

most important in Rousay for thousands of years, with continuous settlement since Neolithic times to the present.

The moorland **Trumland RSPB Reserve** near the pier is a good place to see Hen Harriers, Merlin, Peregrine and Red-throated Divers, while the rare *Primula scotica*

may be found on the maritime heath of the west coast.

Nearby **Wyre** has a 12th century Norse castle, **Cubbie Roo's Castle** and a 12th century Romanesque chapel, both of which are said to have been built by Kolbein Hruga, a colourful character in the *Orkneyinga Saga*.

Egilsay was the site of the martyrdom of Earl Magnus and has the fine 12th century **St Magnus Kirk** with its tall round tower. A cenotaph marks where he is said to have been killed at Easter 1117.

All three islands are reached by ferry from Tingwall in Rendall.

Midhowe broch, Westness, Rousay

Midhowe broch, Westness, Rousay

Midhowe stalled cairn

Westness brooch

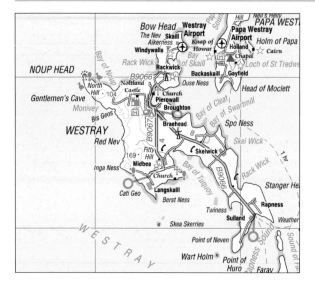

Westray (ON *Vestr-ey*, West Isle), often referred to as *"The Queen of the Isles"*, is the second largest of the North Isles, and in many ways could be described as *"Orkney in miniature"*. The island has dramatic cliffs, good beaches, several ancient monuments, and is the best place in Orkney to see Puffins easily. Westray can be reached daily by ro-ro ferry, or by air.

Noup Head is an RSPB Reserve and a major seabird breeding site

Pierowall has a very good harbour, and was settled in Pictish and Viking times. Norse remains have been found in several places, including here and at Tuquoy Church. There was a Neolithic settlement at the Links of Noltland, near the gaunt 16th century shell of **Noltland Castle**, commenced about 1560 by Gilbert Balfour.

Ruins of several chambered cairns exist, but none are very impressive. At Point of Cott the outline of an excavated cairn can be seen, while a carved stone found at Pierowall is in the Orkney Museum in Kirkwall.

Broch mounds can be seen at **Burrastae** and **Queena Howe**. Westray has been intensively farmed for thousands of years which explains the relative dearth of prehistoric monuments in good condition. Recent excavations at Quoygrew (Norse) and Knowe o'Skea (Iron Age) have thrown some light on the island's past.

The landscape more than makes up for this with the dramatic cliffs at **Noup Head RSPB Reserve,** which is second in numbers of breeding seabirds to St Kilda. In the south the **Castle of Burrian** near Rapness is the easiest place to see **Puffins** in Orkney and during the breeding season this rock stack is home to many of the cheeky little birds.

Sandy beaches are another feature of Westray, with **Grobust** in the north being perhaps the best, but in fact a sheltered beach can be found for every wind direction

Westray and Papay aerial view from the south west, Pierowall lies along the bay at left centre

for picnics. In rough weather it can be very exhilarating to take a brisk walk and watch the waves.

Westray can be visited for a day, but merits at least an overnight stay. The Pierowall Hotel has been recently refurbished and offers *"perhaps the best fish and chips anywhere"*, fresh from the local whitefish fleet, as well as a warm welcome.

Noltland Castle was built about 1560

With its diverse range of habitats, Westray is a good place for the nature enthusiast. With sandy beaches, the maritime heath of the northwest coast with *Primula scotica*, and charming agricultural countryside, the island offers much to birders and botanists.

Pierowall from the south

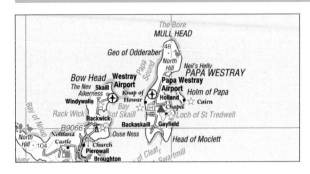

Papay or **Papay Westray**, takes its name from the Celtic clergy who were there before the Vikings. This small island lies just east of Westray, to which it is connected by the **shortest scheduled air route in the world**, a distance undertaken in two minutes or less, depending on the wind.

The **Knap of Howar**, is the oldest known stone built house in Orkney and, like Skara Brae, it was revealed after a severe storm. The walls of the well-preserved houses still stand to a height of 1.6m, and the stone interiors are remarkably intact.

Large numbers of artefacts including much Unstan Ware pottery was found, along with bone, flint and stone tools. Bones of domestic animals, fish, seals and birds, including Great Auk were abundant as well as many mollusk shells.

The earliest dates were from about 3600BC, 500 years before Skara Brae, and the latest about 3100BC, so the site may have been occupied for at least 500 years.

The **Holm of Papay** has two chambered cairns, the larger being of Maeshowe-type with a chamber over 20m long with 12 side cells. This impressive and mostly intact structure is well worth a visit. Teistie Taing at the south end is a good place to see seals and the nearby Bay of South Cruive is good for finding *Groatie Buckies* (Cowrie shells).

Early Christian Sites include **St Tredwell's Chapel**, dedicated to

St Triduana is built on top of an Iron Age broch on the Loch of St Tredwell. Triduana was a nun whose eyes were so admired by Nechtan, King of Picts, that she plucked them out and sent them to him on a thorn branch to retain her virtue.

The **St Boniface Church** near the Knap of Howar has been refurbished and is worth a visit. Boniface was a 7th century English missionary who became Archbishop of Germany in 728AD, and was massacred with his followers in 754AD.

The church dates from the 12th century and is still in use today. The interesting grave yard has an 11th century hog-backed gravestone which has been linked to the burial of Earl Rognvald Brusison in c.1045. This site has extensive Iron Age, Pictish and Norse remains, and there was probably a much older chapel here before the Vikings arrived.

Holland Farm has a fine 19th century steading with a circular horse engine house, doocot and corn drying kiln. The main part of the house dates from about 1636, and there is an interesting folk museum in the bothy.

St Boniface Kirk dates from the 12th century

11th century hog-backed gravestone at St Boniface

The Knap of Howar is the oldest known house in Orkney, and dates from about 3600BC

Wildlife Papay is famous for its birds, with the North Hill being an **RSPB Reserve** and home to many breeding Terns and Arctic Skuas in summer. There is a small bird cliff at **Fowl Craig** on the east side, site of the killing of the last Great Auk in Britain in 1813.

The island is also a good place to search for migrants in spring and autumn. The Mull Head is said to be perhaps the best place for sea-watching in Orkney, as it forms a natural turning point.

Crofts and fields on the east side of Papay

Flora The North Hill is mostly made up of maritime heath and has an interesting variety of plants, many in dwarf form. These include several sedges and herbs such as Dog Violet, Primrose, Spring Squill, Grass of Parnassus, Heath Spotted Orchid, Mountain Everlasting and *Primula scotica.*

The Holm of Papay from the North Hill

Holm of Papay South chambered cairn - interior

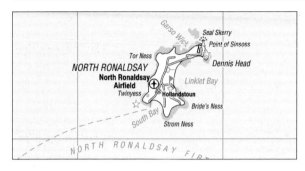

During lambing time the ewes are allowed onto grass for a time, and special sheep punds around the shore are used for clipping and dipping. The white and brown fleeces are fine and suitable for knitwear, but the coloured ones are rather coarse.

Most of the houses are renovated traditional longhouses, while the farming itself tends to be less intensive and more traditional than elsewhere in Orkney. As a result the island is a haven for breeding and migrant birds, and has its own **Bird Observatory**, from where staff observe and record the bird visitors, but also offer human visitors meals and accommodation.

North Ronaldsay is especially well situated on a migration cross-roads for birds on passage to northern breeding grounds in spring and on their return in autumn. A number of rarities turn up every year.

There are several sites of archaeological interest. These include the Iron Age **Broch of Burrian** at the south end, the **Standing Stone** which has a small hole through it

North Ronaldsay (ON *Rinansey*, Ringan's or Ninian's Isle) lies to the north east of Sanday, which it resembles with its low lying landscape and sandy beaches. The island has a distinctly different character, and still retains many traditions and language usages now extinct in most of the rest of Orkney. It is the most isolated of the North Isles and is mostly served by air link.

The **sheep dyke** is a unique feature of the island. This 12-mile drystone dyke was built about 1832 to keep the sheep off the agricultural land. The small, hardy **North Ronaldsay Sheep** are similar to Soay sheep, and graze the seaweed off the shore as well as grass on the small areas outside the dyke. The lean meat has a distinctive flavour because of the unique diet.

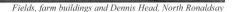

Fields, farm buildings and Dennis Head, North Ronaldsay

North Ronaldsay sheep eating seaweed on the shore

North Ronaldsay sheep

near the pier, and the **Muckle Gairsty**, an ancient "treb" dyke which divided up the island.

North Ronaldsay lighthouse, at Kirk Taing on Dennis Head, was the first in Orkney, and it was established in 1789. This was the only lighthouse in the North Isles until the Start Point light was built in 1806 on Sanday. The Dennis Head beacon was extinguished in 1809 and its light replaced by the ball of masonry removed from the old Start Point beacon. There are ambitious plans to renovate the beacon and associated houses.

Kirk Taing, North Ronaldsay and old lighthouse beacon, built 1789

By 1852 the need for a lighthouse was clear and the new brick-built lighthouse was first lit in 1854. It was the last one in Orkney to be made automatic, in 1999. At 42m it is the highest land-based lighthouse in Britain. Dennis Head lighthouse is open to the public by arrangement. The North Ronaldsay trust owns the lighthouse buildings, some of which now house a small mill to process the local wool. A shop and cafe is open in summer.

North Ronaldsay is good walking country, whether the long walk

Loganair Island aircraft serve North Ronaldsay

around the dyke or the shorter walk to the lighthouse, the island will not disappoint visitors.

Transport While it is possible to reach North Ronaldsay by sea from Kirkwall once a week or on a few trip days in summer, most people travel on the Loganair Islander aircraft from Kirkwall Airport.

Stan Stein - the stone with the hole

North Ronaldsay lighthouse - lamphouse

North Ronaldsay lighthouse

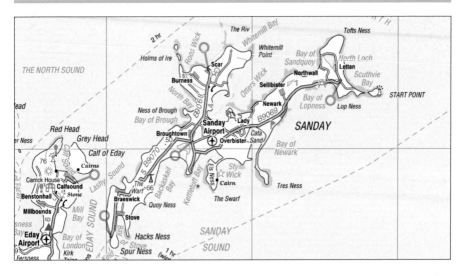

Sanday (ON *Sand-ey*, Sandy Isle) is the largest of the North Isles. It is very low lying, apart from at the south end, and has many beautiful sandy beaches backed with machair. In summer there is a riot of wild flowers, while the shallow sandy bays are a favourite with the many migrant and resident waders.

Although there are many sites of archaeological interest, only the **Quoyness chambered cairn** is actually on display to the public. This impressive Maeshowe-type cairn on the peninsula of Elsness dates from about 3000BC and very much merits a visit.

Sanday was settled before 4000BC, and the early farmers would have found the light soils easy to till. It was also probably the first to be settled by the Vikings for the same reason. Excavations at Pool have shown that occupation was virtually continuous from the Neolithic until post Viking times.

A recent exciting find at Scar was a Viking boat burial, in which three people were interred. A spectacular whale-bone plaque was among the artefacts found. This may be seen, along with other artefacts, at the Orkney museum in Kirkwall.

Start Point lighthouse was first lit in 1806, although an unlit beacon was installed in 1802. The present light was built in 1870. It is painted with vertical black stripes to distinguish it from North Ronaldsay lighthouse, which has horizontal red stripes. Start Island can be reached at low tide by crossing Ayre Sound.

With its flat terrain and lovely shoreline, Sanday is good for bird watching, walking and cycling. The many flat, muddy and sandy beaches, backed by machair, small lochs and marshes are very attractive to waders, both breeders and migrants.

Quoyness chambered cairn, Sanday

Start Point lighthouse, Sanday

Backaskaill Bay

Otters frequent the shores and small lochs, and may be seen in the early morning or late evening. Their presence can be noted from their distinctive tracks and fishy spraints. Many Common Seals live around Sanday, especially off the north coast. Grey Seals breed on the Holms of Ire and Spur Ness.

There are two hotels at Kettletoft for accommodation and meals. Sanday can be reached daily by sea or air from Kirkwall.

Whitemill Bay

Lopness Bay with remains of WW1 destroyer, B98

Whalebone plaque from Scar

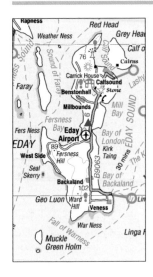

Eday (ON *Eid-ey*, Isthmus Isle) is less fertile than the other outer North Isles and much of it is peaty heather moorland. Its central position means that there are excellent views of much of Orkney from, for example, the top of the Ward Hill, or from Red Head.

The **Stone of Setter** is 4.5m high and very prominent as it is set in open terrain overlooking Calf Sound and near the Mill Loch, in a focal point of the landscape. The weathered monolith is covered in lichen, which emphasises its timeworn appearance.

.

Chambered cairns There are many chambered cairns on the island, some in good condition and some ruinous. **Vinquoy**, is a Maeshowe-type cairn which overlooks Calf Sound. This interesting structure has been repaired and is built of large sandstone blocks. It has two pairs of side chambers and the main chamber is over 3m high inside.

Braeside is a small tripartite cairn whose entrance passage directly faces the Stone of Setter, while the nearby **Huntersquoy** is on two levels like Taversoe Tuick on Rousay. The upper chamber has largely gone, but the bottom one is intact.

Carrick House was first built in 1633 and in 1725 nearby Calf Sound was the scene of the capture by its then owner, James Fea, of "**Pirate Gow**". John Gow was the son of a Stromness merchant, and went to sea. In 1724 he and 5 others mutinied aboard the ship "*Caroline*" off Spain, murdered the officers and proceeded to harry shipping.

Having little success they ended up in Stromness, but the ship was recognised and they sailed to Eday, looking for assistance from Fea, who had been at school with Gow. However Gow and his fellow pirates were captured and he and 7 of his crew were executed in London.

Wildlife The hide on the Mill Loch is a very good place from which to observe Red-throated Divers, and other waterfowl which nest here. Whimbrels, Hen Harrier, Merlins, Arctic Skuas and Short-eared Owls may also be seen on the island during the summer.

The **Eday Heritage Walk** takes in the most interesting sights in the north of the island. It starts at the shop and passes the Mill Loch, Stone of Setter, chambered cairns and Noup Hill, from where there are fine views over the North Isles.

Calf Sound from the east, Carrick House is mid left

Aerial view of Eday and Stronsay from the north west, Holm of Faray and Faray in foreground

The **Warness Walk** does the same at the south end, starting from Backaland Pier going round the southwest part of the island. Both are signposted.

The **Calf of Eday** lies across Calf Sound from Eday. There are several chambered cairns. These include a long stalled cairn, a small two-celled tomb and two intact Bookan-type cairns. Opposite Carrick are the remains of a 17th century salt-works which was peat fired.

Beaches There are also several very nice beaches - at the Bay of Greentoft, at the Sands of Doomy and at the Sands of Mussetter. Mill Bay and the Bay of London are especially good for waders.

Transport Eday can be reached daily by ferry from Kirkwall, and less frequently, by air from Kirkwall Airport.

The Stone of Setter

The Red Head of Eday

Vinquoy chambered cairn

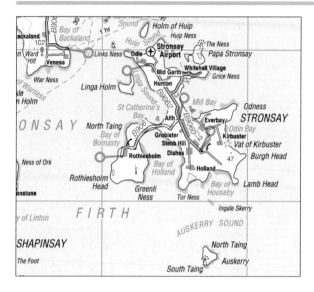

Herring Stronsay was a major centre for Herring fishing for centuries. The Dutch were fishing for Herring in Orkney waters in late Norse times and by the 17th century had over 2,000 boats working the North Sea. The island was used as a harbour for Dutch and Fife boats during the season for hundreds of years up until 1937, when the fishery collapsed due to overexploitation.

Kelp-making was introduced to Stronsay about 1719, to make potash and soda, which were used in glass and soap manufacture and were in short supply due to the American and French Wars.

Stronsay (ON *Strjonsey*, Profit Island) is one of the most fertile islands in Orkney, and has a much indented coastline, with many very fine beaches, as well as low cliffs on the south east side, with several large caves, and a natural arch at the **Vat of Kirbuster.**

Although most of the island is farmland, the large headland of Rothiesholm is mostly moor, thus there is a large variety of habitat and feeding areas for wildlife.

There are a number of archaeological sites on the island, but none of great interest, no doubt because it has been intensively farmed for many years. There is a large chambered cairn at Kelsburgh near the Bu and two smaller ones at Lamb Head.

On **Papa Stronsay**, now occupied by Transalpine Redemptorist monks, there is a chambered cairn the "Earl's Knowe" and a chapel site, St Nicholas. This dates from the 11th century, but the site may go back to the 8th century.

Kelp was produced by burning dried seaweed in pits on the shore. The expansive beaches in the North Isles were excellent sources of seaweed, which had traditionally been carted onto the land as fertiliser, and, at the peak, Orkney was exporting 3,000 tons per year.

The boom lasted from 1780 to 1830, and brought much money in to the landowners, some of which was invested in farm improvements. Kelp pits can be seen at many places round the shore, especially at Grice Ness, east of Whitehall.

Whitehall Village was very busy during the fishing season, and once boasted the longest bar in Scotland. On Sundays there were hundreds of boats tied up; however, the increased catching power of the steam drifter meant that the stocks of herring were exhausted before WW2.

The Vat of Kirbuster - a collapsed cave

Today the harbour is home to a few inshore creel boats. The former Fishmarket has been done up as an interpretation centre, cafe and hostel. The Stronsay Hotel in Whitehall has recently been renovated and offers food and accommodation.

Beaches On Stronsay there is a beach for every wind direction. St Catherine's Bay, the Bay of Holland, the Bay of Huip and Mill Bay have the largest expanses of sand, but there are many other small beaches to explore.

Wildlife Stronsay is an excellent island for birdwatching, being well sited to attract migrants in spring and autumn. The diverse range of habitats attract many unusual species at times.

Grey Seals haul ashore to pup at several places around the island, with large numbers on Links Ness and on Linga Holm, as well as on Grice Ness, Odness and Lamb Head. Common Seals are also .present.

Walking Being flat, the island offers easy walking, with several waymarked official trails. These include Odin Bay to Houseby, Sand of Rothiesholm and Baywest, St Catherine's Bay, Grice Ness and Holland Farm to Torness.

Transport Stronsay can be reached daily by sea and air from Kirkwall.

Stronsay, aerial view from the south

Whitehall Village from the West Pier

Whitehall Village from the East Pier

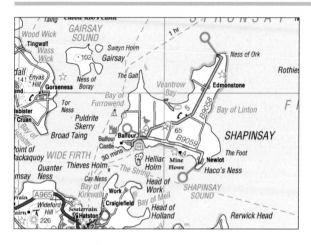

Shapinsay (ON *Hjalpand-isey*, Helping Island) is only 20 minutes from Kirkwall by ro-ro ferry. It was one of the first areas where the old runrig system was changed to larger fields, and is nearly all cultivated today.

The **Broch of Burroughston** is the only archaeological site which is on display, having been excavated in 1862. It is surrounded by a ditch and rampart, and has a well-preserved interior, nearly 3m high inside. There is an intact corbelled cell in the entrance passage and a large central well accessed by steps.

The 3m **Mor Stane** is of indeterminate date and is said to have been thrown by a giant from the Mainland at his departing wife. On the north side below Lairo Water, **Odin's Stone** may have been a Norse meeting place.

Shapinsay featured in the unsuccessful bid by King Haakon of Norway to reassert Norse power in the west of Scotland in 1263. The great fleet was mustered here in Elwick Bay, before its departure for the Clyde.

Balfour Castle The house that is now Balfour Castle was first built

in 1674. In 1775 Thomas Balfour married Frances Liginier, whose money paid for the Sound Estate. Soon the estate was transformed with a new house, Cliffdale, the village, then called Shoreside, farm buildings and dykes all being built.

In 1846 David Balfour, who had made a fortune in India, inherited the estate, which now included the whole island. He had the house transformed into the present building. The Castle and gardens make a very interesting visit today, the interior not being much changed in 150 years, with most of the original furnishing and interior decor still in place.

The disused Elwick Mill is one of the largest water mills in Orkney, and the artificial loch behind it is now the **RSPB Mill Dam Reserve**. Good views of many kinds of waders and waterfowl may be had from the hide on its west side. The small lochs of Lairo Water and Vasa are also good places for birds, while the tidal Ouse and mudflats of Veantrow Bay are good for waders.

Dishan Tower and Balfour Castle, Shapinsay

Sunset over the Wide Firth

Elwick Bay and Balfour Village, with Balfour Castle in the background, Shapinsay

Beaches The island boasts a number of fine sandy beaches, including Skenstoft, Sandside, Innsker, Noust of Erraby and Sandy Geo on the north side. The best is probably the south-facing Bay of Sandgarth in the southeast corner of the island, said to be the Shapinsay folk's favourite.

Transport Shapinsay makes a pleasant short excursion from Kirkwall. The Castle and gardens are open regularly, there is an excellent restaurant, the Smithy and a pub in the village.

B&B accommodation is available on the island.

Burroughston Broch

The Mor Stane

Balfour Village Harbour and MV "Shapinsay"

81

MV "Hrossey" at Hatston Terminal, Kirkwall on a midsummer evening

GETTING TO ORKNEY

Although apparently isolated and far away, Orkney is in fact very well served by transport links, both by air and sea. There are good daily year-round connections by air from all four major airports in Scotland and by ferry to Caithness. Ferries to Aberdeen and Shetland run several times per week.

Land travel to the ports is facilitated by good roads as well as bus and rail services which tie in with some ferry times. Contrary to the advice given by some travel agents, no passport is needed by UK citizens, prices are reasonable, and there are a variety of services.

AIR Today it is not necessary to go to the lengths that the first airborne visitors had to. In 1910, the author's grandfather was surprised to find two young Germans from Munich on his doorstep. They had gone for a flight in their balloon, hoping to reach Switzerland. Much to their consternation the weather changed and they crossed the North Sea, landing at the back of Park Cottage, Kirkwall, after seeing the lights of the town!

British Airways operate several flights into Kirkwall Airport (KOI) every day, through its francise partner, Loganair, from Aberdeen, Inverness, Edinburgh and Glasgow. There are also daily flights to and from Shetland. Saab 340 aircraft which carry 34 passengers with a cruising speed of 250kt at 20,000ft are used. Kirkwall Airport is open seven days per week and is equipped with an Instrument Landing System, which has greatly improved reliability of flights in poor visibility.

Flight details, information and bookings can be found online, or by calling British Airways.
Tel 0870 850 9850 (24 hours)
www.ba.com
Information can also be had from the BA desk at Kirkwall Airport.
Tel (01856) 873611

Ridgway Travel, 67-69 Albert Street, Kirkwall, Orkney KW15 1HQ, the local travel agent, will also be delighted to help with travel arrangements to and around Orkney.
Tel (01856) 873359
Fax (01856) 872680
www.ridgwaytravel.co.uk

SEA Regular sea links to Scotland have been operated for many centuries. Today the main routes are from Stromness to Scrabster, St Margaret's Hope to Gills Bay and Kirkwall to Aberdeen and Lerwick. There is a lso a passenger ferry in summer from Burwick to John o'Groats. All sailings are subject to weather conditions, and disruption due to storms can occur in winter especially.

Loganair SAAB 340 in British Airways colours at Kirkwall Airport

NorthLink operate *MV Hamnavoe* between Scrabster and Stromness which takes about 1½ hours to cross the Pentland Firth, passing the Old Man of Hoy on the way. She crosses at least twice daily, and carries up to 180 cars and 500 passengers. NorthLink also operate *MV Hjaltland* and *MV Hrossey*, between Aberdeen, Kirkwall and Lerwick. These vessels call several times per week all year round.

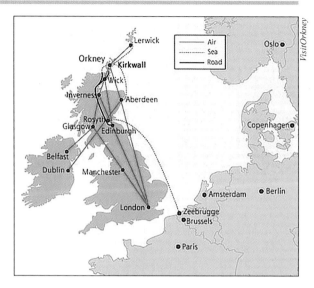

The Smyril Line vessel *MV Norröna* provides connections to the Faeroes, Iceland, Hantsholm and Bergen. This vessel now calls at Scrabster and Lerwick during the summer.
NorthLink Ferries Ltd, Kiln Corner, Ayre Road, Kirkwall KW15 1QX
Reservations 0845 6000 449,
Tel (01856) 885500
Fax (01856) 879588
www.northlinkferries.co.uk

Pentland Ferries operate year-round services from St Margaret's Hope to Gills Bay in Caithness. The trip takes about 1 hour and there are three services per day. From spring 2008 a catamaran with a passenger capacity of 350 will operate the route with a crossing time of 45 minutes.
Pentland Ferries Ltd, Pier Road, St Margaret's Hope, Orkney KW17 2SW
Tel (01856) 831226
Fax (01856) 831614
www.pentlandferries.co.uk

John o'Groats Ferries operate a summer passenger service between John o' Groats and Burwick in South Ronaldsay. Coach services meet the sailings at Burwick for transport to Kirkwall, while there is a special bus service from Inverness to John o'Groats. Several variations on day trips are available.
John o'Groats Ferries, John o'Groats, Caithness KW1 4YR
Tel 01955 611353
Fax 01955 611301
www.jogferry.co.uk

Getting to Scrabster The A9 trunk road north from Perth is not a good road, and it takes about 6 hours to drive the 250 miles north from Edinburgh or Glasgow. The part north of Inverness is very scenic but windy and can be very busy in summer.

There are plenty of good hotels and B&Bs to stay in Caithness overnight, and indeed some time exploring this area is strongly recommended.

MV "Hamnavoe" in Hoy Sound on a "coorse" day

John o'Groats Ferry "Pentland Venture" in harbour

BUSES AND TRAINS

Land transport links from Edinburgh and Glasgow to Aberdeen and Thurso are operated by Scottish Citilink and by First ScotRail. Details of services and timetables are available from the companies.

Scottish Citilink Coaches Ltd, Buchanan Bus Station, Killermont St, Glasgow G2 3NP
Tel 08705 505050
Fax 0141 332 4488
www.citylink.co.uk

ScotRail Railways Ltd, Caledonian Chambers, 87 Union Street, Glasgow G1 3TA
Tel 08457 048 4950
www.scotrail.com

The Orkney Bus is operated in partnership with John o' Groats Ferries, and runs daily from Inverness and to John o'Groats and back when the ferry is running.
Tel: 01955 611353
www.jogferry.co.uk

Rapsons claims to be Scotland's largest independent coach operator and run services all over the Highlands, 1 Seafield Road, Inverness IV1 1TN
Tel (01463) 710555
Fax (1463) 711488
www.rapsons.com

Connections There are coach connections between Thurso train station and Scrabster as well as between Wick and Gills Bay. Citilink buses also meet

some sailings of the *Hamnavoe*. It should be noted that the timetables are not always synchronised and thus it is important to check out such expected connections in advance. All of the times may be checked out on the websites listed here.

PRIVATE CAR From Edinburgh or Glasgow it is about 40 miles by motorway to Perth, from where Inverness is 114 miles and should take roughly two hours, through some of Scotland's most spectacular scenery. The A9 should be tackled with care, patience and attention as it can be very busy. There are many good viewpoints and places to stop for a meal.

From Inverness to Scrabster is 111 miles. This road takes about 2 hours and offers many good stop-off opportunities at the attractive towns, villages and sites of interest along the route. When time allows, a slightly more leisurely journey can become a delightful part of the Orkney experience.

Stroma lighthouse

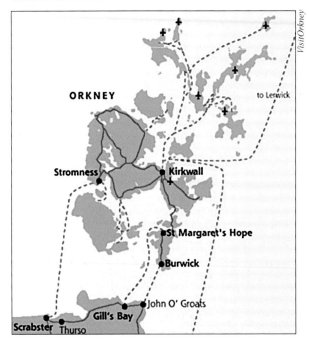

VisitOrkney

ORKNEY

Stromness

Kirkwall

St Margaret's Hope

Burwick

John O' Groats

Gill's Bay

Scrabster Thurso

to Lerwick

All services are ro-ro except those to Papay, North Ronaldsay and Graemsay, where vehicles are handled by crane. The modern fleet of ships runs frequent daily services to all islands except North Ronaldsay, which is once or twice weekly. The services run as follows:

Outer North Isles services depart from Kirkwall for Westray, Papa Westray, Eday, Sanday, Stronsay and North Ronaldsay. To book telephone (01856) 872044

Rousay, Egilsay & Wyre services depart from Tingwall in Evie. To book telephone (01856) 751360

Hoy and Flotta services depart from Houton in Orphir. To book telephone (01856) 811397

North Hoy & Graemsay services depart from Stromness. To book telephone (01856) 850624

Fares. There are two levels of fares to the islands. Tickets for the inner islands of Hoy, Flotta, Rousay, Egilsay, Wyre and Shapinsay are cheaper than those to the Outer Isles of Westray, Eday, Sanday, Stronsay and North Ronaldsay. There is a discount available for 10 journey tickets. Since these apply to all islands in the same price band it is quite easy to use up 10 tickets in a holiday!

A trip to Orkney is not complete without a visit to one or more of the islands, as well as visiting all the interesting places on the Mainland. Since each island is different, with its own charm and the inter-island transport system is good, it is both easy and interesting to visit all of the islands as well as the Mainland parishes.

INTER-ISLAND SEA TRANSPORT The main internal sea transport operator is Orkney Ferries, which operates to most inhabited Islands from Kirkwall, Tingwall, Houton and Stromness. They publish an annual timetable with details of services. Further information from the head office at Kirkwall Harbour Tel (01856) 872044

MV "Eynhallow" on her way to Rousay from Tingwall

"No visit to Orkney is complete without a visit to one or more of the islands on our ferries."

"Steeped in history, surrounded by Beauty"

ORKNEY FERRIES Ltd

Shore Street, Kirkwall KW15 1LG
Tel 01856 872044 Fax 01856 872921
www.orkneyferries.co.uk
info@orkneyferries.co.uk

"No Orkney holiday would be complete without visiting the many beautiful islands in the group. Jump on the ferry and travel back in time where seals, wildlife and an abundance of archaeological sites and a wealth of scenery await."

We operate seven ferries between the Mainland and thirteen of the inhabited smaller islands, with daily sailings to most. Be sure not to leave Orkney wishing that you had gone on an island trip.

For bookings please refer to the telephone numbers opposite

Call us today for your free colour brochure and details of our reasonable rates for sailings, mini cruises and package tours.

A Loganair "Islander" aircraft in Highland Park livery

BOAT HIRE Several independent operators have boats available for hire for sightseeing, sea angling, etc.. Please ask at the Tourist Office or locally for the latest information.

INTERNAL AIR SERVICES Loganair run daily services to most of the Outer North Isles, including Westray, Papay, North Ronaldsay, Sanday and

Passenger view aboard an "Islander"

Stronsay and to Eday on Wednesdays only with 8-seat Islander aircraft. Flying from Kirkwall airport, this service is very popular, and booking is generally required.

Special deals exist for visitors, including the *Coast to Coast* ticket which allows visits to up to three islands at a very special price. One island is accessed by sea and

two by air. Tickets are available from the Orkney Ferries office only.

Bookings and Enquiries:
Tel (01856) 872494/873457
Fax (01856) 872420
www.loganair.co.uk
or the local travel agent,
Ridgway Travel,
Tel (01856) 873359
Fax (01856) 872680

It should be noted that flights to North Ronaldsay are frequently very busy so to avoid disappointment book well in advance.

PUBLIC TRANSPORT Rapsons are the main bus operators in Orkney, and run a large number of services between Kirkwall and Stromness, to ferry terminals and various locations on the Mainland.

Full details of all these and other schedules are published by Orkney Islands Council every six months in the **Orkney Public Transport Timetable**. This booklet is indispensable to anyone wishing to make best use of the complexity of routes and times.

Car Hire Orkney is very much a car-orientated society, and independant transport makes it much easier to see the areas not served by public transport. Several firms have cars for hire, including on many of the islands. In particular a car is essential to reach many of the most interesting places as public transport only serves the main population centres and sites of interest.

Taxis Taxis are available throughout Orkney, either for normal hires, or tours. See advertisements for telephone numbers. Please check in *"The Orcadian"* or ask at the Tourist Office for further information. There are taxi ranks at the Harbour, Broad Street and the Airport in Kirkwall and in Stromness at the Pier Head. Taxis may also be ordered to meet ferries, etc.

Bicycle Hire Orkney, being relatively flat, is good country for cycling - but note the wind direction before setting off - it could be much harder getting back! While the main Kirkwall to Stromness road can be rather busy,

A Rapsons coach crosses Churchill Barrier #3

there are many secondary roads which are very quiet. On a nice day there is no better way to absorb the rhythm of the countryside than from a bike. Bikes may be hired in Kirkwall and in Stromness as well as on several of the islands.

Tours of Orkney Apart from the Maxi Tours offered by John o'Groats Ferries, many smaller operators offer tours on the Mainland and several of the islands. Discover Orkney Tours (01856) 872865 and Wildabout (01856) 850583 offer tours suitable for small groups. Traveller Guide on Rousay (01856) 821234 and

Westraak on Westray (01857) 677777 do guided tours on these islands.

Roving Eye Enterprises (01856) 811360 do cruises on their vessel *"Guide"* in Scapa Flow with an underwater camera, where non-divers can get sub-aqua views of the WWI German ships.

There are many other small tour operators on various islands so check out with VisitOrkney, or, locally.

A Loganair "Islander" aircraft

Scapa Flow sunset from Burray

St Mary's, Holm

Whitemill Bay, Sanday

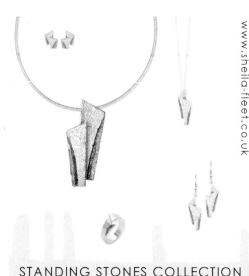